A Lover Repents

(A Husband Confesses His Sin)

Published by:
Be Broken Ministries
San Antonio, Texas
www.bebroken.com

Printed in the United States of America

Table of Contents

WHAT IS A LOVER REPENTS?

The words to follow are written as the heart cry of one man. It is provided as an opportunity to peek into his journey. This writing shares how one man struggled with his past addiction to pornography, how that man struggled in crying out to God, and how that man grieved for his wife and the impact his addiction had on her.

The husband in this story wrestles with these thoughts,

- "How do I apologize? I'm sorry is not enough."
- "I have caused a deep wound, an emotional violation."
- "I've rocked her sense of well-being."
- "She now doubts where she was once confident."

Writer's Note:
Just because this is a raw confession of one man, the reader should not assume that the husband is completely in the wrong and the wife is completely flawless. The reader is encouraged to use this writing to better understand the male struggle.

Note to Readers:
If you would like a sneak peak at how this material has impacted other readers, go to the Feedback section at the end of this booklet.

THE FORMAT

This material occurs in sexual dialogues listed below. Here is an overview of each section. The sections are labeled "pleas." Here is the outline.

1. A Plea of Admission:

"One man, this has been my struggle."

A husband talks to God about his sexual secret.

2. A Plea of Openness:

"I see my sins glaring before me."

He realizes his sins have hurt others.

3. A Plea of New Insight:

"She is the daughter of the King."

A husband has his eyes opened. He recognizes a spiritual truth. His wife is God's daughter.

4. A Plea of Confession:

"Father, I need to confess to you."

A husband confesses. He takes ownership of his sin.

5. The Plea of A Troubled Spirit:

"I had two dreams."

The Father speaks to this husband through dreams.

6. The Plea for Healing:

"Please heal her as You have healed me."

The husband has matured, after experiencing God's love he wants the same for his wife.

7. The Wife's Plea:

"His wife shares from her heart."

8. A Plea for a Prayer:

"How shall I pray?"

1. A Plea of ADMISSION

THIS HAS BEEN MY STRUGGLE.

A husband talks to God about his sexual secret.

I am an average American male.

I'm married, have a job and am a Christian.

Many of you know me.

I see you every Sunday.

I attend worship and Sunday school.

My involvement with church goes way back.

However, I have a secret.

My wife doesn't know.

My close friends don't know.

My parents don't know.

This secret invades every crevice of my head.

It is there in the morning when I rise.

It gnaws on my brain as I drift off to sleep.

No one knows this part of me.

I have a sexual playground in my mind.

This playground has grown over the years.

It started when I was a young man.

An older man's sexual fantasy material, porn, was dumped in the middle of my young, innocent mind.

It grabbed me.

First, shock.

Then, stunned.

Overwhelmed, emotions and adrenaline surged simultaneously.
It was like nothing I'd ever felt before, exciting, but wrong.

First, it grabbed me.

Then, I grabbed back.

I quietly pursued it.

It was my secret tool to assist during the hard times.
It filled lonely spaces.
It distracted me from anxious moments.
It took me away from hard reality.
If delivered momentary comfort.

It has left me feeling divided and full of shame.

I have tried to stop my escape into sexual fantasy.
I promised myself that I would quit at least 100 times.
And, I have started again at least 101.

I want to be a 100% disciplined Christian man. Life's failures, rejections, and disappointments happen and I run to the sexual playground in my head for comfort.

I cannot get myself free. I tried. I prayed. I wanted. I started. I cried out to Heaven.

Over time the struggle only seems to have gotten worse.

I cannot battle myself and win!

It is as if in the division, I developed two minds.
One mind loves good, God and right.
The other mind loves fantasy pleasure.

Today, I plan to have a face to face with Jesus.
I must simply put it all out before Jesus today.

2. *A Plea of OPENNESS*

"I SEE MY SINS GLARING BEFORE ME."

He realizes his sins have hurt others.

Father,

I need to talk to you.

There is something weighing heavy on my heart.

It occupies a sad place.

It gnaws on my spirit.

It eats at my soul.

Like King David, "my sin is ever before me."

You know everything.

There are no secrets hidden from you.

But I still need to share something.

As I begin to confess,

I cannot even look at you.

I must bury my face in my hands.

I am brokenhearted.

I have wounded my wife, your daughter.

What you wanted me to do,

I did not do.

Instead, I did what I wanted.

I bow before you with one request.

I plead to you.

Please heal the wound I created.
I am asking you, my Father.
You the great Physician.
You have the power to create with one word.
With one word you can nurture a soul.
One of your words can mend a broken heart.
I entreat you, Father.

I am talking about your daughter.
I want her to know love again.
Love her in the wounded places.

But how can I take back what I have done?
How can I be part of the healing?
What can I say but
"I am sorry."
"I am **so** sorry."

What can I do?
I am deeply grieved.
She trusted me.
She placed her hopes and dreams in me.
All she wanted was a healthy, safe relationship.
She is such a romantic.
She is a true lover.

And I was a stupid young man.

My focus was on me, and what I could get.

She trusted me.

In turn, I wounded her spirit.

Once discovered, my secret sexuality left her in shock and disbelief.

She spent evenings crying.

And she cried alone.

I know she grieved deeply.

What could she say?

Who could she tell?

In that moment there was only grief and despair.

I left her steeped in confusion and uncertainty.

I know you have a vision for your daughter.

I know you wanted her to be safe.

She had dreams.

She had visions of a wonderful life.

And she saw me as part of Your plan.

I destroyed that vision.

As a young girl she would lay in bed and dream.

She loved movies about love and romance.

She heard fairy tales about knights and heroes.

And on her life journey,

She ran into a selfish, adolescent man instead.

I am on my knees, Lord.

I am begging you.

Renew her heart.

Restore her innocence, please.

Father,

Could you heal and restore wounded places in your daughter?

Can you free her mind and heal her heart?

Can you restore innocence and purity?

I know I am not the only one who has wounded her.

Can you restore the dreams spoiled by rude, selfish men?

Please Father,

I am asking you to restore her,

help her dream again.

Father,

I need to confess.

I have been unfaithful, if only in my thought life.

I lied!

I manipulated!

Now I hide my face

as Adam hid his face in the garden.

I know now I hurt your daughter.

Forgive me.

Please Lord, forgive me...

3. A Plea of NEW INSIGHT

"SHE IS THE DAUGHTER OF THE KING."

The husband has his eyes opened. He recognizes a spiritual truth.

His wife is God's daughter.

I know how much you love your daughter.

She is a daughter of the King, living in submission to you.

She is a lover of Your truth.

Her heart beats for you, her designer.

She submitted herself.

She followed the desires of her heart.

She submitted to this relationship.

She trusted me. I betrayed her.

You trusted me. I betrayed you.

Your daughter is a reflection of you.

She is a lover.

She is not a sexual object or fantasy.

She is not a toy.

She is your lovely creation.

She aspires to beauty and has love in her soul.

Ultimately, she is designed to be your lover.

You alone complete her.

You will never fail her.

You dearly love her.

She is a gift to a chosen husband,

She is perfectly designed to grow a great marriage.

4. Plea of CONFESSION

"FATHER, I NEED TO CONFESS TO YOU."

A husband confesses. He takes ownership of his sin.

Father,

Allow me to continue to confess.

I have come to see your daughter differently,

I see her as one who provides laughter, kindness and care.

Father,

I failed you.

I failed myself.

I failed your daughter.

I failed my family and Your church.

I have failed.

I bury my face in shame.

I cannot face you.

My pillow is wet with tears.

I acknowledge your words.

I know from Your Word that,

"In the end it would be better for that person to be thrown into the

sea with a large stone

around his neck than to cause harm to Your beloved."

This is the fate for those who would hurt your precious daughter.

I must make amends.

I fear the day I meet You face to face.

You are a God of judgment. You are a God of righteous anger.

Forgive me.

Please Lord, Forgive me.

I know You made Your daughter for good works.

You designed her to be a giver.

Her heart overflows with love, and

Her heart is filled with hugs.

Hopes and dreams fill her mind.

She desires a pure life of dedication,

unsoiled, unstained, unblemished.

All she wanted was a White Knight,

a good man, a faithful husband.

She wanted romance.

She dreamed of finding a protector.

Then I entered the picture.

Me,

a selfish adolescent in a man's body.

She wanted a dream.

When we married, I was ignorant in youth, surging in biology, and
absorbed in self.

It was all about me.

Her hearts' desire was to be honored and cherished.

She longed for the special man.

Forgive me.

Please Lord, forgive me!

I wish Your daughter could see the battle within myself.

I am full of torment.

Frustration.

Failure.

Shame.

She would see periodic steps towards self-control followed by
frustration.

Then, a heart cry;

a new start, a new prayer, a new promise.

More failure.

Repentance, more effort to try, followed by more failure.

She would see a young man tormented between
submission and selfishness.

My raging battle spilled out and wounded your daughter.

Forgive me.

Please Lord, forgive me.

Father,

Your eyes look into the soul.

You know Your daughter;

her personality and character,

her strengths and weaknesses.

You know her likes and dislikes.

You knit her together in her mother's womb.

You knew all her days before she came to be.

You have loved her from the cradle

And you will continue loving her to the grave and beyond.

I grieve, knowing I robbed her of something special.

I shattered innocence.

I weakened her self-worth.

I opened the doors of doubt and fear.

Forgive me.

Please Lord, forgive me.

Father,

Please release her from the pain my ignorant behaviors inflicted.

I left a residue of shame on Your daughter.

At times, the lust within me would not be bridled.

Forgive me.

Please Lord, forgive me.

Lord,

Her beauty is designed for your eyes.

She is yours.

She was not mine to take.

She was adorned for Your eyes.

Her innocence and youthfulness were yours.

My flesh tormented me.

I did not bridle my sexual fantasies.

I fed those thoughts.

My sexual appetite shouted.

The lie consumed me.

My fantasies overwhelmed me and made me their fool.

They did not deliver all they promised.

My sexuality promised fun.

Instead, it has become my tormentor.

A moments pleasure grew into a lifetime of secrecy, shame and

guilt.

I am now a divided man.

Torn between following God and letting my flesh lead.

I brought shame on myself, my family, and You.

If lashes would restore her innocence,

then I would say, "Whip me."

If denying my body food would give her back what I took,

then I would say, "Starve me."

My mind searches for a way to right the wrong.

I can only say words.

But You can heal hearts, minds and souls.

Father,

I have grown,

Now I have a daughter.

Now I know what I did.

Your daughters are your prized possessions.

They spin and swirl.

They dance and sing.

They are full of energy, passion and delight.

They are a reflection of your goodness.

I am here today, not for me.

I have come to ask for restoration of Your daughter.

I come before you with a broken and contrite spirit.

Lord, I come with heaviness in my heart.

I am here on her behalf.

She does not know I am talking to you.

My heart understands.

Sorrow rises.

I am filled with sorrow, shame and guilt.

Forgive me...

Please Lord,

      forgive me.

You challenged me to stand before You blameless.

I followed the culture, buying the lies.

I fear I have left her wounded in spirit,

heavy-hearted,

emotionally closed off,

bitter and broken.

Father, forgive me.

Lord, I want to clean up the mess I have made.

I want to make amends for my selfish sin.

I want to help restore your daughter's simple, pure innocence.

Restore her heart.

Make it new again.

Allow her to drink deeply of your healing.

5. *The Plea of a TROUBLED SPIRIT*

"I HAD TWO DREAMS."

The Father speaks to this husband through dreams.

Lord,

Last night I had two dreams.

I fear you sent them.

In the first dream,

I was overpowered by a brilliant light.

It knocked me to the ground.

I could not see.

Then I heard a stern, troubled voice,

    "You know my daughter.

    She is precious in my sight.

    You caused her pain. You caused her to doubt her value,

    worth, and beauty.

    You did not only wound her,

        you have deeply wounded <u>Me</u>."

My heart sank...

Sadness flooded in...

I could only manage these words,

"Is that you, Lord?"

    "Yes!"

I began weeping and could not stop.

I could barely gasp for breath.

The story of Paul on the road to Damascus flashed before me.

Blinded, Paul heard Christ saying, "Why do you persecute me?"

The Father's words resounded again.

They thundered in my ears.

> "You have deeply wounded Me.
>
> Your offense is against me. I cherish my beloved.
>
> I desire her to be bathed in love and security."

I could not answer. I could only weep.

In the second dream,

It was Judgment Day.

I was walking toward the gates of heaven, my mind remembering past failures.

Bad habits raced before me.

My lying and deceiving flashed past.

Times I failed and did not care were brought to mind.

I knew in a moment.

I prepared a speech.

"Father, I have failed you in so many ways.

Let me explain..."

I walked closer.

I passed through a thin mist.

Then,

there you were sitting on your throne,

surrounded by splendor.

I crumbled before you.

I fell to my knees.

I could not speak.

When you spoke there was only one question.

No social greeting.

No small talk.

Rather, with your heavenly voice you asked

one resounding question,

"How did you treat my daughter?"

I was stunned.

Then, more questions,

"Did you take care of her?

  Did you treat her well?

  Did you unconditionally love her?

  Did you sacrifice for her?

  She is my precious one, my beloved daughter."

All remaining air was sucked out of my lungs.

I could not breathe.

Those questions were never expected.

I dropped lower.

I buried my face in the dirt.

Gasping.

Stunned.

Suddenly and uncontrollably my mind started to race.

I was forced to remember times when my sexuality went unbridled
and my thoughts went unchecked.

Then,

You spoke again.

This time there was judgment in your voice.

"As you treated my daughter, so you have treated me.

  Let your own behavior be your judge."

Next, I saw myself

tied in ropes made of my lies, manipulation and shame.

Dragged away I heard your last words,

"Tie a heavy stone around his neck and cast him into the sea of
fire."

The dreams awakened me.

I sat up in bed sweating,

Shaking.

I jumped out of bed and landed on my knees.

There was only one place to run.

Burying my face, and crying out in my spirit,

I repeated the words of the blind man on the road to Jericho.

"Jesus, Son of David, have mercy on me!"

"Jesus, Son of David, have mercy on me!"

Help me!

Forgive me!

Mercy! Mercy!

I prayed and searched.

I knew the promises.

Slowly, Bible verses and hymns rose up in my mind and heart.

"If the Son sets you free, you are free indeed."

And,

"He has taken our sins away from us, as far as the east is from the
west."

"Though your sins be as scarlet, they shall be as white as snow."

Then more,

"Come to me, all you who are weary and heavy laden, and I will give you rest."

My mind was determined to cling to these words,
Pushing out all other thoughts.

"He offered himself once and for all times, the perfect sacrifice."

"He came to give his life as a ransom for many."

Then I heard Christ's words,

"No one here condemns you. Go and sin no more."

In that moment, I was reminded the Father sent the Son.
He sent His Son as a healing balm for wounded hearts.
Not just for my own personal redemption, but for all who need restoration from past hurts.

He sent his Son to *heal me* and *restore his wounded daughter*.

Thank You Jesus!

Exhausted and comforted, I crawled back into my bed and drifted off to sleep.

My spirit rejoicing with an old Christian favorite:

On a hill far away stood an old rugged cross,

the emblem of suffering and shame;

and I love that old cross where the dearest and best

for a world of lost sinners was slain.

So I'll cherish the old rugged cross,

till my trophies at last I lay down;

I will cling to the old rugged cross,

and exchange it some day for a crown...

My final thought as I drifted back to sleep,

     His grace covers me...

6. The Plea of HEALING

"PLEASE HEAL HER AS YOU HAVE HEALED ME."

The husband has matured, after experiencing God's love he wants the same for his wife.

God,

Why is growing up so hard?

       "Me, all about me."

       What was I thinking?

My sins stare at me.

They mock me.

My sins challenge me.

These sins are the footprints of my ignorance and selfishness.

I do not cry for myself.

I cry for my wife, for innocence lost, for promises broken.

Purity tarnished,

Dreams dashed,

Holiness mocked.

I am asking for healing and restoration.

Father forgive us for our stupidity and heal the scars left on your daughters.

My heart cry is for restoration.

Please Father,

Do not let a wounded heart hinder my wife's walk.

Do not let cynicism keep her from healing.

She hopes and dreams and loves.

Restore any damage done to her heart.

Oh God, only you can soften a hardened heart.

Give my wife what you have given me.

Shame is falling off.

My sins are removed as far as the east is from the west.

My journey began with woundedness. My solution was porn. The
result left me trapped and my wife cheapened.

Lord,

> You are healing me.
>
> One day at a time.
>
> Today, I am walking in Heaven's design.

I have sinned.

My father has sinned. My father's father has sinned.

Break the curse.

Begin with me.

Restore my wife so she can sing, dance and freely love You again.

Thank you Lord, for teaching about true love. Amen.

7. The WIFE'S PLEA

"HIS WIFE SHARES FROM HER HEART."

Some time has passed since I have learned about my husband's secret sexual thought life. Here is the prayer from my brokenness.

Father,

My childhood was good. I was a blessed little girl, loved and protected by my father and mother. Protected, sheltered and trained up in the way a child should go, I have loved you Lord. My heart was pure and my dreams big.

In my teenage years I stayed faithful and continued to share, serve and pray. Love grew. Hope swelled. My nighttime prayer was, "Lord, I wait on your will. Patiently wait for my prince and the happy life I know you have planned for me."

As a young girl I read of knights, heroes, Prince Charming and sacrificial love. My imagination built up dreams of tall and handsome, chivalrous and smart. A man who would love me and my God. I knew you were preparing a loving Christian for me.

I was fortunate to marry a good man. He has a good heart. I know he loves me.

However, soon after the "I DO!" the sparkle and dreams faded. Living a normal, average life was the reality. I have accepted my life. But, a recent discovery has crushed me. I have discovered my husband's secret life. He recently confessed to me a past of ongoing porn use and a sexual history I never knew.

I am wounded and crushed. I don't understand. How could this happen?

My First Response,
CONFUSION, CHAOS and PAIN

How could this happen? I don't deserve this. God, I am angry at my husband and you. What happened to my happily-ever-after life? I have lived according to your laws. I have been patient, practiced self-discipline, and denied myself. Now I feel cheated. My heart has been damaged. My own self-worth comes into question.

Why? Why couldn't I be enough? Why didn't he stop after we married? Why did he marry me? Why wasn't I good enough? Why wasn't I woman enough? Why wasn't I attractive enough?

How could he do this? Why didn't he stop himself? How could he risk throwing everything away? Why couldn't he control himself?

My love story has become a story of damaged love and a wounded heart.

I wanted a dream relationship.

A relationship full of

>Desire

>Innocence

>Growth

What I got was ache.

>Heart ache

>Body ache

>Spirit ache

I have had my own opportunities to betray, yet I remained faithful.

I feel betrayed.

>Vulnerable

>Wounded

>Confused

I have so many questions and so few answers.

>Does he love me?

>Did he ever love me?

>Why did he marry me?

Thinking and rethinking, I always come to the same conclusion.

I cannot make things right again.

Life will never be the same.

Exhausted from asking "why?" and finding no satisfactory answers.

I am drowning in questions. And all his answers fall short.

God has had me on difficult journeys before. I need to remember past lessons.
Lord, remind me of your faithfulness.

My Second Response,
I NEED A BIGGER PERSPECTIVE. I NEED A HEAVENLY VIEW.

In the midst of all this pain and confusion I ask myself,
What do I know?
I need answers bigger than myself and my husband.

Here is what I know:

> God is God.
> He is still good and faithful.
> The Bible still contains the truth.
> And I am still your daughter, Heavenly Father.

I have my shortcomings in this marriage. I am by no means the perfect wife. However, in my marriage I have not developed an elaborate, secret, sexual life full of lust.

> God, I know you still love me.
> And you have not failed me.

You long to nurture me and care for me. You have a vision for me, even in this pain.

My Heavenly Father and I are okay.

My husband is the mess.
He is the one with the secret sexual thought life, now exposed.
He is the one who thought he could bridle lust and fantasy without consequences.

However, he is now learning the eternal lesson, "The truth will find you out."

Father,

My husband is bringing forth past struggles and issues.
I feel overwhelmed, disappointed and flooded with grief.
I am in the midst of the valley of the shadow of death.
However, my spirit whispers a reminder, "You are more than your feelings."

Through humiliation, shame and disrespect you are with me.
When I feel lied to, cheapened and taken advantage of,
You are with me.

Finally,

DEEP WITHIN ME I HAVE A PEACE. AND I KNOW IT IS
WELL...

Even in my loss I have hope.

In my mind and spirit I have found peace.

One thought resonates-

      I have walked alone before. And you are *always* with me.

Thank You that no matter what life throws at me,

what struggles I face,

how others disappoint me,

what valleys I walk through,

I will remember,

      You are *always* with me!

Father,

I take great comfort in knowing it is well between you and I.

However, my marriage is a wreck.

The relationship needs a lot of work.

Help me accept my husband's apology.

Help me to heal. Help him to heal.

I found trusting is risky and I'm still scared.

Help my husband to work on emotional and spiritual growth.

Help me to understand the sexual struggles of a man.

There is a long road ahead but I know you are with me.

Father I love you,

    Your daughter

8. Plea for a PRAYER

"FATHER GIVE ME A PRAYER"

As I sit here and pray quietly, my mind wants to wander. Fears rise and doubts stir. I am crying out to you Father, seeking your voice. I need a prayer to focus my mind.

In the midst of the chaos and confusion swirling through my mind I hear a still, small voice, whispering words of comfort from the Old Testament.

> "The Lord is my shepherd; I shall not want.
> > *(Some days I feel like a sheep, lost and in need of a shepherd.)*
>
> He makes me to lie down in green pastures;
> > *(but some days my plan is to throw a fit, kick and stomp.)*
>
> He leads me beside the still waters. He restores my soul;
> > *(There are days I need soothing, restful waters.)*
>
> He leads me in the paths of righteousness For His name's sake.
> > *(My path has not changed. I am still called to follow Him along the pathway of righteousness. I still bless Him and His holy name.)*
>
> Yea, though I walk through the valley of the shadow of death,

(Death seems to have come near. My ideals for my marriage, husband and future are now dead.)

I will fear no evil;

(Evil does not win. Evil may not have me, my husband or my marriage. I will not walk in fear and confusion.)

For You are with me; Your rod and Your staff, they comfort me.

(I need your comfort. I need your rest. I need your presence.)

You prepare a table before me in the presence of my enemies;

(You are my feast. You fill my spirit. You satisfy me.)

You anoint my head with oil; My cup runs over.

(You bless me. My bounty comes from you! Good is from you alone. You provide me with new dreams, rising from the ashes of the old.)

Surely goodness and mercy shall follow me all the days of my life;

(Goodness does follow me. God blesses me. The Lord showers new mercies upon my family.)

And I will dwell in the house of the Lord Forever."

(NIV)

The prayer continues with words from the New Testament.

Our Father in heaven,

  (Dear Father,)

hallowed be your name,

  (Bless your holy name.)

your kingdom come,

  (Bring your kingdom to earth. Establish your reign in my heart.)

your will be done on earth as it is in heaven.

  (May your will be done here on earth, as it is in heaven.)   *(NLT)*

Give us today our daily bread.

  (Give me the provisions I need for each day.)

Forgive us our debts,

  (Forgive me of my sins.)

as we also have forgiven our debtors.

  (Help me to forgive those who have sinned against me.)

And lead us not into temptation,

  (Do not let me yield to difficult temptation.)

but deliver us from the evil one.

(Save me from Satan and his deception.)

(NIV)

Finally, I pray for a release. Letting go of all the bitterness eating away at me, I pray for a grateful heart.

"Lord, I am so tired. Pain and anger have been slowly eating away at me. I am tired of being so full of hatred.
This hostility is slowly stealing my life. I have become bitter and mean. My heart is empty of everything but resentment.
How can I get rid of this?"

I chose a grateful heart. I chose to turn and embrace the Lord, thanking Him for His perfect plan. I do all this in submission, despite an unwilling heart. I know that in thanking the Lord, He will return my joy. The joy stolen by the enemy and his work.
I know that when I embrace gratitude (allowing my heart to be full of gratitude) there is no room for resentment, bitterness, or a desire to 'get even.' I model the spirit of Christ, allowing my heart to be full of gratitude."

Why a spirit of gratitude?

The New Testament shares with us that gratitude is the solution to bitterness:

- Jesus gave thanks before he fed the 5,000.

- He gave thanks before calling Lazarus up from the grave.

- He also gave thanks as he broke the bread in preparation for going to the cross.

The Lord brings to my mind words from Paul. His instruction to the Thessalonians was to have a grateful heart.

A. Give thanks in all circumstances, for this is God's will for you in Christ Jesus. NIV

B. Be thankful in all circumstances, for this is God's will for you who belong to Christ Jesus. NLT

C. In everything give thanks; for this is God's will for you in Christ Jesus. NAS

D. Whatever happens, give thanks, because it is God's will in Christ Jesus that you do this. (God's Word)

   1 Thessalonians 5:18

Father, guide me on this difficult journey.

Help me to see you as my leader and shepherd.

Help me to see you as my kind, loving Father.

Help me to find gratitude in the midst of pain and confusion.

I love you Father,

   Your daughter.

Feedback:

#1 "This was very strong and I am grateful to have read it. Thank you so much. One of my immediate responses is "I never repented that strongly for my sexual sin -- or anything else!" But the work encourages me, saying: _Join right in. Read me aloud if you wish, read me alone to yourself or to your wife._" (male reader)

#2 The sense of poetry is good. I think it reaches the soul at a deeper level and suggests further that a man and woman can take it in each on their own, or together." (male reader)

#3 "I appreciate the rawness and honesty of the wife's plea. Many, many women will be able to relate."

#4 "Tears came to my eyes as I read the feelings of the wife. My husband and I are very grateful to have taken part in this reading. It is not for a fresh wound but for a made up heart it is great healing. I brought out the transcript and showed it to my husband. We read this as a husband and wife of God. The Holy Spirit came in and soothed my husband and I with openness and brokenness." (female reader)

#5 This echoes my heart and my feelings, it also helped me understand a little bit about what was going on in my husbands mind. (female reader)

#6 "I absolutely loved it and needed this. There are so many people struggling on both sides with this, that this type of stuff is needed so badly. So I am a fan, eternally grateful for this work." (female reader)

#7 "Thank you for sharing this story of guilt, shame, and repentance. I know first hand how devastating sexual sin is when the secret is found out. Every day is a struggle to honor the man given in marriage with respect especially when you find nothing respectable about him. I had to fight to be able to open my heart to love again, knowing that unconditional love was never in the mix. (female reader)

#8 "Thank you for this husband's prayer and supplication for all men struggling with sexual sin. It affirms to me that there is still hope for these men to grow in mature faith. I felt every emotion this wife has gone through and continue to repent of my own struggle with hurt and bitterness this marriage has grown in my heart. This reading helped me to remember I must look to my husband as a man and fix my eyes on whatever trace character qualities that may indeed reflect Christ." (female reader)

#9 "Thank you again for sharing this story. I am so glad I am not alone." (female reader)

#10 "I was impressed with the writing of this material. It truly depicted what a woman feels and is going through when the Lord reveals to her about her husband's secret sexual sin. I was also able to glimpse the sorrow and understanding from a man when he realizes what his secret sexual sin has caused not only to himself but also to the others around him." (female reader)

#11 "This material has helped me as a wife with a husband struggling with sexual addiction to understand his struggle to have hope that someday he will understand the gravity of what this sin inflicts on those he professes to love. Thank you so much for letting me read this material." (female reader)

#12 "The vulnerability and desperation of the heart of *A Lover Repents* was portrayed honestly. The words allowed me the insight of a glimpse of the heart of my husband.
The pain I have experienced in this journey has consumed me. At times I have been overwhelmed by one sentence, one thought, or one moment. I found the poetry style pertinent in the expression of emotion." (female reader)

#13 "Many of the words clearly expressed the emotions I have felt as a wife of a man who has chosen pornography over intimacy. Pain, repentance and hope are woven into the Pleas of *A Lover Repents*. I can truly relate to response of the wife." (female reader)